12/09

THE REVOLUTIONARY WAR LIBRARY

The Brave Women and Children of the American Revolution

JOHN MICKLOS, JR.

Enslow Elementary

an imprint of

Enslow Publishers, Inc.

40 Industrial Road
Box 398
Berkeley Heights, NJ 07922
USA

http://www.enslow.com

Frontispiece: Betsy Ross and her daughter show the first American flag to George Washington and other Continental officials.

Enslow Elementary, an imprint of Enslow Publishers, Inc.

Enslow Elementary® is a registered trademark of Enslow Publishers, Inc.

Library of Congress Cataloging-in-Publication Data

Micklos, John.
   The brave women and children of the American Revolution / John Micklos, Jr.
      p. cm. — (Revolutionary War library)
   Summary: "Learn how the women and children kept life going, spied, and fought in the Revolutionary War"—Provided by publisher.
   Includes bibliographical references and index.
   ISBN-13: 978-0-7660-3019-0
   1. United States—History—Revolution, 1775-1783—Participation, Female—Juvenile literature.
2. United States—History—Revolution, 1775-1783—Women—Juvenile literature. 3. United States—History—Revolution, 1775-1783—Participation, Juvenile—Juvenile literature. 4. United States—History—Revolution, 1775-1783—Children—Juvenile literature. 5. Women—United States—History—18th century—Juvenile literature. 6. Children—United States—History—18th century—Juvenile literature. 7. Spies—United States—History—18th century—Juvenile literature. I. Title.
   E276.M53 2008
   973.3082—dc22
                              2007048510

Printed in the United States of America.

10 9 8 7 6 5 4 3 2 1

To our readers: We have done our best to make sure all Internet Addresses in this book were active and appropriate when we went to press. However, the author and the publisher have no control over and assume no liability for the material available on those Internet sites or on other Web sites they may link to. Any comments or suggestions can be sent by email to comments@enslow.com or to the address on the back cover.

Every effort has been made to locate all copyright holders of material used in this book. If any errors or omissions have occurred, corrections will be made in future editions of this book.

♻ Enslow Publishers, Inc., is committed to printing our books on recycled paper. The paper in every book contains 10% to 30% post-consumer waste (PCW). The cover board on the outside of each book contains 100% PCW. Our goal is to do our part to help young people and the environment too!

Illustration credits: Courtesy Sharon M. Foster, p. 35; The Granger Collection, pp. 6, 13, 34; The Hermitage: Home of President Andrew Jackson, Nashville, TN, p. 21; Independence National Historical Park, p. 16; Hulton Archive/iStockphoto, p. 32; Bill Manning/iStockphoto, p. 40 (Betsy Ross house); Library of Congress, pp. 1, 4, 10, 12 (top), 17, 18, 19, 20, 24-25, 26, 28, 31, 33 (top), 38, 40 (Boston Tea Party), 41 (Molly Pitcher, Surrender of Cornwallis, Deborah Sampson); Courtesy of Morristown National Historical Park, p. 33 (bottom); National Archives and Records Administration, pp. 27, 41 (Treaty of Paris, Battle of Savannah); Courtesy National Park Service, Museum Management Program and Guilford Courthouse National Military Park, GUCO1492 (flax comb), p. 12 (bottom), GUCO1652 (niddy noddy), p. 5 (top), GUCO1569 (thimble), p. 7; Courtesy National Park Service, Museum Management Program and Morristown National Historical Park, MORR3499 and MORR3501 (saucer and handleless teacup), p. 11, MORR3986 (portrait brooch of Captain Daniel Parker), p. 15; North Wind Picture Archives, pp. 30, 36; Photos.com, pp. 5 (bottom), 8; used under license from Shutterstock, Inc., pp. 9, 14, 22; The Putnam Foundation, Timken Museum of Art, San Diego, p. 39.

Cover Photo: Courtesy Deborah Johnson (background soldiers); Library of Congress (Betsy Ross)

Produced by OTTN Publishing, Stockton, N.J.

TABLE OF CONTENTS

CHAPTER ONE

The Roles of Women and Children

"Washed . . . Ironed . . . Scoured rooms . . . Pulled radishes . . . Killed the pig . . . Made bread . . . Made 5 shirts for the doctor . . . did other things."[1] This entry from the diary of Mary

In colonial America, women had many tools to help them with their daily duties. A niddy noddy (right) was used by colonial women to measure yarn for weaving.

Women used spinning wheels (bottom) to turn wool, cotton, or flax into thread and yarn. These materials could then be used to make clothing.

Holyoke provides a glimpse at women's work around the time of the Revolutionary War. Life was hard.

Women worked hard, but they had few rights. For the most part, they could not vote. Women rarely owned homes or businesses. Husbands owned all the property. When they died, the family's land passed on to their sons.

Few married women held jobs outside the home. Their job was to run the house, take care of the children, and help

their husbands. Women rarely had any time to relax. Each task had to be done by hand. There was no electric power or running water.

The proper role for a woman, people of the time thought, was to be a wife and mother. Women who did not marry were called spinsters. People looked down on them.

Married women spent much of their lives having and raising children. Some women had a baby every couple of years over a period of twenty years or more. Having children was dangerous. Most babies were born at home. If

Women in colonial America were expected to marry and have children. Childbirth was dangerous. When the Revolutionary War broke out, there were fewer than 200 men in the thirteen colonies who had medical degrees.[2] Many women and babies died during childbirth.

★ ★

FUN AND GAMES

Most children had little time to play. Many of their games were simple ones that did not need much equipment. Children played hopscotch, leapfrog, and hide and seek. Some flew kites, played marbles, and jumped rope. Popular toys included tops and dolls.[3]

there were any problems, both mother and child were at risk. Often, women died in childbirth. Many children died young, too.[4]

Even if they survived, children lived a hard life. After infancy, they were treated as little adults. Even young children did chores. They fetched water and cleaned the house. They fed the farm animals. Most children had little time for play.

Many communities worked to provide schools. But few children

A brass thimble like this was part of every woman's sewing kit.

Women often had duties on the farm in addition to their household responsibilities. This drawing of women working alongside slaves on a southern tobacco plantation was made around 1750.

had a chance to attend. They had to work around the house or farm. Those who did attend often found that the school lacked supplies such as books and writing tools.

At the age of fourteen or so, many boys became apprentices. This meant that they were training to learn trades. Three important trades were blacksmith, shoemaker, and cooper. Blacksmiths made items of metal. Coopers made barrels and other wooden containers. As apprentices, boys often learned to read, write, and do math. These skills were part of the business.[5]

Most girls were taught at home. Many parents thought it was more important for girls to spend time doing household chores than to spend time in school.[6] In many homes, mothers taught their daughters to read and write.

A young man who wanted to become a blacksmith typically had to serve an apprenticeship of four to seven years.

Some girls learned a lot this way. Others learned very little. It all depended on how much their mothers knew and how much time they had to spend teaching.

Most women from wealthy homes did receive an education. Some went to school. Others had private teachers. Some women, such as Abigail Adams, wanted more women to get an education. Abigail often talked to her

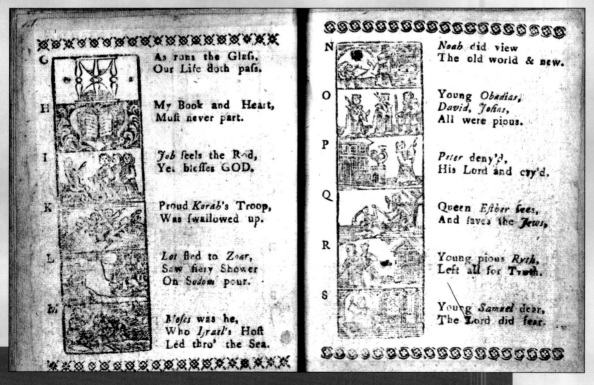

The *New England Primer* was a textbook used by some American students. These illustrated pages teach the letters *G* through *S*.

This teacup and saucer were made in China for a wealthy woman who lived in the colonies during the war. Most American families could not afford such fine household items.

husband, colonial leader John Adams, about women's rights. These included the right to education and the right to vote.

During the time leading up to the war, women's roles began to expand. Many women became active in the protests against English taxes. In 1767, the British passed a law called the Townshend Act. This act taxed goods imported, or brought over, from England. In protest, many colonists boycotted. They did not buy British goods.

This British cartoon from 1774 (left) pokes fun at a group of American women who have agreed to boycott English tea.

American women used wooden combs (bottom) to soften a plant called flax, so that it could be woven into cloth. Making clothing from flax meant that Americans did not have to buy linen cloth from Great Britain.

Some women gathered for "spinning bees." There they wove cloth by hand. This meant they did not have to buy the cloth from England. By doing so, they were helping "the public good," wrote one newspaper.[7] Later, women helped support the boycott of English tea. They did the shopping, and they refused to buy tea.

★ ★ ★ ★ ★ ★ ★ ★ ★ ★ ★ ★ ★ ★ ★ ★ ★ ★ ★

WOMEN IN BUSINESS

Some women did run businesses, either on their own or on behalf of their families. Before the Revolutionary War, when she was still a teenager, Eliza Lucas Pinckney ran three plantations. Over the years, she became wealthy.

Benjamin Franklin traveled often. While he was gone, his wife, Deborah (pictured), ran his printing business. She also helped run the postal service after Ben was made postmaster for the colonies.

Women lacked legal rights, but many wives held the real power in their homes. In most cases, their husbands spent their days working. They spent evenings with other men talking about relations with England. In the meantime, their wives controlled the household. They ran the homes and raised the children. They made the day-to-day decisions. The men handled global affairs. "The women," one writer noted, "handled pretty much everything else."[8]

CHAPTER TWO

Holding Down the Home Front

"Here I sit on Buttermilk Hill

Who can blame me, cry my fill?

And every tear would turn a mill,

Since Johnny has gone for a soldier."[1]

This song, popular during the war, sums up how many families felt. Fighting raged from 1775 to 1781. Many men enlisted in the army. Some served only a few months. Others served through the entire war.

With husbands away fighting, women's burdens grew. They continued to run the homes. They cooked, cleaned, and raised the children. Often they had to run their husbands' farms or businesses, too.

Over time, women began to feel some ownership. Early in the war, Mary Bartlett wrote to her husband about the status of "your farming business." After a couple of years, she began to refer to it as "our farming business."[2]

People who lived in areas where fighting took place faced even greater problems. Armies from both sides often took over private homes. They camped on the land. Sometimes they even made families take

Some women's jewelry was painted to show their soldier husbands. This brooch (pin) pictures a Continental Army captain.

officers into their homes. Soldiers raided people's livestock and gardens. In the South, the British sometimes took slaves with them when they left an area.[3]

Eliza Wilkinson reported that the British took all her extra clothes. They even took the buckles from the shoes she was wearing.[4] When a British officer took over the home of Elizabeth Drinker of Philadelphia, she complained that he moved in with "3 horses, 2 cows, 2 sheep, and 2 turkeys." He even brought his servants.[5]

Poet Ann Eliza Bleecker suffered even more. She left her home in northern New York as British general John Burgoyne's army approached. She feared the British would harm her and her infant baby, Abella. She took her daughter and fled to the woods. The baby died of cold and hunger.[6]

Women did more than just support the war effort through their work at

In her day, Annis Boudinot Stockton was a well-known writer. Her patriotic poems convinced many people to support the cause of independence.

American women helped the war effort by knitting clothes for the Continental Army.

home. Many helped in other ways. To help clothe the soldiers, some states set quotas. Cities had to provide a certain amount of clothing for the troops. In 1776, women in Hartford, Connecticut, had to make 1,000 coats and vests and 1,600 shirts.[7]

In 1780, Esther De Berdt Reed of Philadelphia wanted to raise money for the patriot cause. She gathered a group of thirty-six women. They went door-to-door

In September 1776, after the battle of Brooklyn Heights, British troops were pursuing the retreating Continental Army. A wealthy American woman named Mary Murray invited the British commander, Lord William Howe, and his officers to stop for lunch at her home. Murray, a patriot, wanted to give the American soldiers time to get away. Her plan worked. The British officers spent the afternoon at her home, and the American army escaped.

collecting money. Within a month, they had gathered thousands of dollars.

The women wanted General George Washington to give the money to his soldiers. Washington had other ideas. He wanted the money used to make shirts for the soldiers. He even asked the ladies to make these shirts themselves in order to save money. By December 1780, the ladies had made 2,000 shirts. They told the general, "We wish them to be worn with as much pleasure as they were made."[8]

Children, too, took on added responsibility because of the war. If their fathers were away fighting, they did tasks such as plowing. They also helped even more with household chores. This gave the women more time to run the family's farm or business. Many children had to cope with the loss of a loved one killed or captured in battle.

In some cases, children saw the war up close. On September 11, 1777, eight-year-old Sarah Frazer was sent

WOMEN'S RIGHTS

In 1776, John Adams went off to Philadelphia. There he helped prepare the Declaration of Independence. His wife, Abigail, urged him to "remember the ladies."[9] She hoped that ladies would soon have many of the same rights men did. Throughout her life, Abigail kept speaking out for women's rights. Change was a long time coming, however.

home from her school in Thornbury, Pennsylvania. British troops were nearby. Soon the Battle of Brandywine began along a creek west of Philadelphia. Her mother rushed off toward the battle to check on Sarah's father. He was a colonel

LEGENDARY FLAG MAKER

Betsy Ross sat sewing in her shop one spring day in 1776. As the legend goes, three men entered. One of them was General George Washington. The men told her they wanted her to make a flag. They showed her the basic design for a flag with stripes and six-pointed stars. The legend says she suggested that the stars have five points instead. She showed them how such stars could easily be made. She went on to make that first flag and many others during the war.[10]

Did Betsy Ross really sew that first flag? Some experts think she did. Others disagree. We do know that Betsy Ross made many early flags in her home on Arch Street in Philadelphia. She ran her flag-making business for more than fifty years.

In April 1781, British soldiers barged into the South Carolina home of fourteen-year-old Andrew Jackson. After the teenager refused to polish a British officer's boots, the officer slashed him with a sword. Jackson, who would grow up to become the seventh president of the United States, bore the scars from this attack for the rest of his life.

in the Continental Army. Colonel Persifor Frazer survived the battle unharmed. Soon after, however, the British captured him. He spent the winter in a British prison. Like many other families, the Frazers had to cope on their own.[11]

CHAPTER THREE

Following the Army

Many women and children traveled with one of the armies during the war. These people were called "camp followers." Some experts estimate that as many as 20,000 women traveled with the

Continental Army over the course of the war.[1] Some women followed the army because they had no homes. Others were unable to maintain the homes they had while their husbands were away fighting. If they stayed on their farms or in their homes, they faced loneliness or even starvation.

Often camp followers were refugees who fled as the enemy army approached. They feared being harmed by enemy troops. About three-fourths of Boston's civilians

★★★★★★★★★★★★★★★★★★★★★★★★

NURSING THE WOUNDED

During the war, more soldiers died from illness than in battle. Diseases such as smallpox killed many troops. Many other illnesses resulted from poor sanitation in camps, as human waste was often not disposed of properly.

Some women served as nurses in the army. Often nurses were more like servants. They scrubbed floors, cooked meals, and washed dishes. In 1777, nurses earned eight dollars per month. General Washington wanted to hire more nurses and pay them better. Having more female nurses would free up male nurses to serve in battle. His idea was not acted upon.[2]

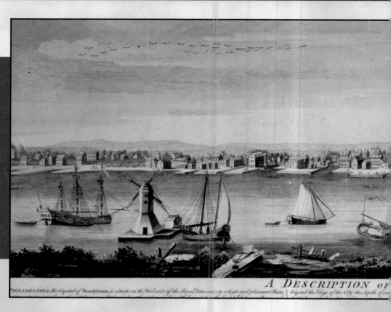

A view of Philadelphia, the largest city in the American colonies during the Revolutionary War. When the British captured the city in 1777, many patriot families fled. Some ended up following Washington's army.

A DESCRIPTION OF

fled the city—which was controlled by the British army— soon after the war broke out in 1775.[3] Likewise, many left Philadelphia when the British took over the city in 1777. For days, wagons left town "filled with household goods and people in flight."[4] Some of them ended up as camp followers of Washington's army.

General Washington realized the value of camp followers. But he also thought they slowed the army down. In 1777, he urged his officers to "get rid of all such as are not absolutely necessary."[5] He also said that women were to travel at the rear of the army with the baggage. He did not want them riding in the supply wagons.

THE SITUATION, HARBOUR &c. OF THE CITY AND PORT OF PHILADELPHIA.

The British army had camp followers, too. In fact, by 1781, the British had one woman for every 4.5 soldiers.[6] This was more than the Continental Army had.

Camp followers provided needed services for the army. Just washing the soldiers' clothes was a huge job. Women earned money for their work. They did not earn much, though. In 1780, at one American camp, women earned two shillings per shirt.[7] That was equal to just a few cents.

Women camp followers also helped the army in other ways. Some served as nurses. Others cooked. "It would not do for men to fight and starve, too," wrote Sarah Osborn, a cook for George Washington's army.[8]

★ ★ ★ ★ ★ ★ ★ ★ ★ ★ ★ ★ ★ ★ ★ ★ ★ ★ ★

MARTHA WASHINGTON

The most famous spouse to stay with the Continental Army was Martha Washington. She did not travel with the army year round, as some women did. However, each winter she left the comfort of her home at Mount Vernon, Virginia, to be with her husband and his troops. She helped cheer up the soldiers during the long winter at Valley Forge. She visited sick soldiers in their huts. She also took charge of the meals at George Washington's headquarters.[9]

Martha did not enjoy camp life. She found the sounds of war frightening. "I confess I shudder every time I hear the sound of a gun," she later recalled of joining her husband with the army for the first time.[10] Still, she stayed. Her presence made life easier for George.

Camp followers had a hard life. Other people looked down on them. One woman described British camp followers as poor, dirty, and smelly. The group included

Generals' wives often joined their husbands during the winter months, when the fighting usually stopped. In this drawing, two of the wives (standing near the house) watch the Continental Army train at Valley Forge.

"some very young infants who were born on the road, the women [in] bare feet, clothed in dirty rags."[11]

Children suffered in this life. They had no real home. They had to travel wherever the army traveled. They could not always get food rations or fresh water. In winter, shelter could be hard to find.

Still, many families lived this way during the war. They had no other choice.

CHAPTER FOUR

At the Battlefront

High above the Hudson River north of New York City, the defenders of Fort Washington prepared for battle. They were surrounded. The rest of the Continental Army had been driven away.

Among those inside the fort on November 16, 1776, were John Corbin and his wife, Margaret. John fired a cannon during the early part of the battle. Margaret helped him load the weapon. Then he fell dead, struck by British cannon fire.

Margaret stepped into John's place. She began to load and fire the cannon herself. Then she, too, was wounded by

MOLLY PITCHER

The legend of Molly Pitcher sprang from the Battle of Monmouth in June 1778. General Washington's troops fought the British on a steaming hot day. According to legend, Mary (Molly) Hays carried water to the troops in a pitcher throughout the battle.

Molly's husband fired a cannon. In between carrying water to thirsty men and carrying water to cool down the cannons, she helped pass the cartridges. One soldier later wrote that an enemy cannonball passed right through her legs, tearing away part of her dress. She kept working. Other versions of the legend have her taking over the cannon after her husband is killed by enemy fire.

Many historians say that "Molly Pitcher" did not really exist. The name referred to "the many women who carried water to cool down the cannons so that soldiers could reload and fire them again."[1]

British cannon fire. She was captured but later released by the British. Her wound caused her to lose the use of her left arm. She received a pension from the army because of her injury.[2] (A pension is a sum of money paid regularly to someone for past service.)

Private Robert Shurtleff drilled, marched, and fought. In one skirmish he was slashed by a saber. In another, he was shot in the thigh. He served bravely for about eighteen months. Then Robert came down with a bad fever. He was taken to a hospital. There the doctor discovered that Robert had a secret. "Robert" was really a woman named Deborah Sampson.

The doctor sent Sampson to General Washington. Washington gave her a discharge. Years later, he invited her to come to Congress. Congress gave her a pension and some land.[3] After the war, Sampson traveled around giving lectures.

A statue of Deborah Sampson, who served with the Continental Army while disguised as a man. Sampson spent about eighteen months in the army.

Elizabeth Zane became a hero by avoiding enemy fire to bring gunpowder to the Americans defending Fort Henry, Virginia, in 1782. The gunpowder enabled the American soldiers to hold out until reinforcements could arrive.

At the end of her speech, she marched across the stage in her old army uniform.[4]

Several other women also fought disguised as men. Sally St. Clair kept her secret throughout the war until she was killed in battle. A few women whose secret was exposed were treated with scorn. Many men thought women should stay at home, not fight in battle.

Only a few women fought in the war. However, many young boys did. Technically, boys under the age of sixteen were not allowed to serve in the army. In reality, many signed up. Some did so to fight for their country's freedom. Others sought adventure. Still others wanted the modest enlistment bonus—twenty dollars, a new suit of clothes, and one hundred acres of land if they enlisted for the entire war.[5]

Peer pressure convinced some young boys to enlist. Fifteen-year-old Joseph Plumb Martin thought of his friends who had joined the army. He heard stories of battle told by

★★★★★★★★★★★★★★★★★★★★★★

FRONT-ROW SEAT TO HISTORY

Many boys and young men served in the army during the Revolutionary War. Few witnessed as many key events as John Greenwood. He joined the army at the age of fifteen. He served during the siege of Boston in 1775 and 1776. Then he took part in the American invasion of Canada. He returned to join Washington's troops in the stirring triumph at Trenton.

Later in the war, Greenwood served at sea. He helped capture several British ships.

Teenager John Greenwood accompanied the Continental Army during the attack on Trenton in December 1776.

After the war, he opened a dental practice in New York City. In the 1790s, he made false teeth for President Washington.[6]

Many young men served in the Continental Army as drummer boys.

other soldiers. All this, as he put it, began "to warm my courage."[7] Martin enlisted in 1776. He planned to spend six months in the army. Instead he ended up serving throughout the rest of the war.

Teenager Ebenezer Fox was serving as an apprentice barber when the shop owner was drafted. The owner convinced Fox to go in his place. Boys such as Martin and Fox were by no means the youngest fighters. David Hamilton Morris joined the army at age eleven.[8]

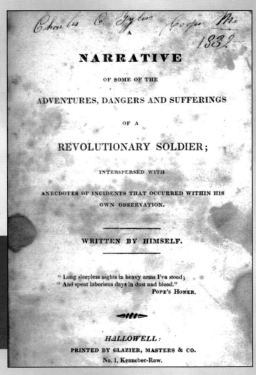

In 1830, Joseph Plumb Martin published a book about his adventures during the Revolution. Martin was a teenager when he joined the Continental Army.

CHAPTER FIVE

Spies and Messengers

The rider sped through the dark April night. At each door, the rider warned that British troops were coming. The militia needed to turn out. It sounds like the famous story of Paul Revere, but it is not.

It is the story of Sybil Ludington. The sixteen-year-old girl traveled the roads of Putnam County, New York, in April 1777. She alerted the militia that British troops were moving toward Danbury, Connecticut. They planned to destroy the arms depot there. The British did destroy the arms, but the militia then helped drive the troops away.[1]

Other women, too, did daring deeds during the war. In Georgia, a slave known as Mammy Kate rode fifty miles to visit her master.

A statue of Sybil Ludington, the teenage girl who warned the New York militia about a British attack in April 1777.

He had been captured by loyalists and placed in jail. He feared being killed. Mammy Kate smuggled him out of jail in a laundry basket.[2]

In South Carolina, a young girl named Emily Geiger was carrying a written message from General Nathanael Greene to another American general. When she was captured

Taverns and inns were popular meeting places for soldiers. For that reason, they were also good places for spies. Women who served food and drink to soldiers might overhear valuable information about troop movements or battle plans.

★ ★ ★ ★ ★ ★ ★ ★ ★ ★ ★ ★ ★ ★ ★ ★ ★ ★ ★ ★

A BIG BANG

Some women spied and carried messages for the army. Others stored guns and gunpowder. In South Carolina, Martha Bratton had supplies and ammunition hidden in her home. The British found out. They sent loyalists to seize the supplies.

Bratton laid a trail of gunpowder from the supplies to a spot outside her home. When the loyalists arrived, she lit the gunpowder. Moments later, a huge explosion destroyed Bratton's home. She was willing to pay that price to keep the supplies out of British hands.[3]

by the British, Emily tore the paper into small pieces. Then she ate them before the British could find anything. After they released her, she rode on and told the general the message.[4]

Men, women, and children alike served as spies. Nathan Hale became the war's best-known spy, even though he was captured and killed. Just before he was hanged, he is said to have spoken the famous words, "I only regret that I have but one life to lose for my country."[5]

Women and children made good spies. They could quietly gather and deliver information. Few people suspected them. They came up with clever ways to pass on what they had learned. One woman sent messages by the way she hung her laundry. A woman named Lydia Darragh sent coded messages hidden in her son's coat buttons.[6]

THE OVERHEARD PLANS

America hung on by a thread at the end of 1777. The British held Philadelphia, America's capital. They took over many private homes, including the home of Lydia Darragh. Washington's army, stationed a few miles outside of town, was weak. One blow might finish the Americans. In early December, the British planned a surprise attack.

Darragh listened outside the room where the British were meeting. She overheard their plan. The next day she sneaked out of town. She made sure the news reached Washington. When the British attacked, they found the American troops ready. The British quickly fell back.[7]

Margaret Gage was married to General Thomas Gage, commander of the British army in the colonies during the early days of the Revolution. Some historians believe she may have spied for the Americans before the battles of Lexington and Concord.

The British had spies, too. One of the best was Ann Bates. She was fearless. One time, she managed to get right inside Washington's headquarters. There she was able to find out about his army's troop strength, along with the number of cannons they had.[8]

General Washington thought that spies were very important. He formed a large spy network. His spies helped him throughout the war. And many of his best spies were women and children.

They joined other brave women and children who wanted freedom for their country. These patriots helped the United States win its independence.

REVOLUTIONARY WAR
TIMELINE

Betsy Ross's house
in Philadelphia

In 1767, the British pass the Townshend Act, which places taxes on many goods imported from England. In protest, many colonists boycott British goods. In some areas, women gather to make goods to replace the imported items that are no longer available.

War begins in April with battles at Lexington and Concord in Massachusetts. Many women watch their husbands march off to war. They are left to tend the family farms and businesses in addition to running the household.

According to legend, Betsy Ross receives a visit from General Washington, who asks her to make a flag for the Continental Army.

The British defeat American troops at the Battle of Brandywine on September 11. They soon capture Philadelphia.

The British turn back an American assault at Germantown on October 4.

| Prewar | 1775 | 1776 | 1777 |

In 1773, colonists rebel against taxes on tea. Again, women have an important role in the protests.

Many young boys, including John Greenwood, enlist in the Continental Army.

Abigail Adams urges her husband, John, to "remember the ladies" when he and other leaders meet to frame the Declaration of Independence.

In November, Margaret Corbin is injured while fighting at the battle of Fort Washington in New York. She later receives an army pension.

On October 17, a British army surrenders in Saratoga, New York.

Lydia Darragh of Philadelphia smuggles out details of a planned British surprise attack on the American troops at Whitemarsh. Because of her spy work, the Americans are ready. The British attack fails.

The Boston Tea Party, December 1773

Battle of Savannah

Camp follower Sarah Osborn, a cook for General Washington's army, witnesses the victory at Yorktown in October 1781.

Cornwallis surrenders at Yorktown

Deborah Sampson

France signs a treaty of alliance with the United States and declares war on England.

Disguised as a man, Sally St. Clair dies in fighting at the Battle of Savannah in 1779. She had kept her secret throughout the war.

Deborah Sampson, who had fought for about eighteen months during the war disguised as a man, gives lectures around the country describing her experiences.

1778 | 1779–1780 | 1781–1783 | Postwar

The legend of Molly Pitcher begins after the Battle of Monmouth in June. Mary (Molly) Hays is said to have carried water to the troops throughout the battle and to have fired an American cannon after its regular crew was injured or killed.

In 1780, Esther De Berdt Reed, wife of the governor of Pennsylvania, and other women raise thousands of dollars for the Continental Army.

In 1783, the Treaty of Paris is signed, officially ending the war. The British recognize American independence.

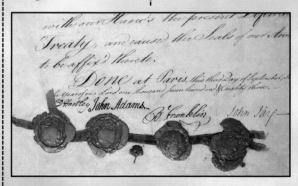
The last page of the Treaty of Paris, which ended the war.

CHAPTER 1: THE ROLES OF WOMEN AND CHILDREN

1. Carol Berkin, *Revolutionary Mothers: Women in the Struggle for America's Independence* (New York: Knopf, 2005), p. 8.

2. Thomas Fleming, *Liberty! The American Revolution* (New York: Viking, 1997), p. 28.

3. Dale Taylor, *The Writer's Guide to Everyday Life in Colonial America From 1607–1783* (Cincinnati: Writer's Digest Books, 1997), p. 137.

4. Cokie Roberts, *Founding Mothers: The Women Who Raised Our Nation* (New York: HarperCollins, 2004), p. 13.

5. Taylor, pp. 236–237.

6. Alice Morse Earle, *Child Life in Colonial Days* (Stockbridge, MA: Berkshire House Publishers, 1993), p. 90.

7. Ray Raphael, *A People's History of the American Revolution: How Common People Shaped the Fight for Independence* (New York: The New Press, 2001), p. 108.

8. Roberts, p. 14.

CHAPTER 2: HOLDING DOWN THE HOME FRONT

1. Carol Berkin, *Revolutionary Mothers: Women in the Struggle for America's Independence* (New York: Knopf, 2005), p. 31.

2. Ray Raphael, *A People's History of the American Revolution: How Common People Shaped the Fight for Independence* (New York: The New Press, 2001), p. 114.

3. Berkin, p. 34.

4. Sally Smith Booth, *The Women of '76* (New York: Hastings House, 1973), p. 259.

5. Berkin, p. 35.

6. Ibid., p. 37.

7. Raphael, p. 118.

8. Ibid., p. 116.

9. Cokie Roberts, *Founding Mothers: The Women Who Raised Our Nation* (New York: HarperCollins, 2004), p. xvi.

CHAPTER NOTES

10. John Balderston Harker, *Betsy Ross's Five Pointed Star* (Melbourne Beach, FL: Canmore Press, 2004), pp. 37–38.

11. Wayne Bodle, *The Valley Forge Winter: Civilians and Soldiers in War* (University Park: The Pennsylvania State University Press, 2002), pp. 78–79.

CHAPTER 3: FOLLOWING THE ARMY

1. Carol Berkin, *Revolutionary Mothers: Women in the Struggle for America's Independence* (New York: Knopf, 2005), p. 52.

2. Oscar Reiss, *Medicine and the American Revolution* (Jefferson, NC: McFarland & Company, Inc., 1998), p. 45.

3. Ray Raphael, *A People's History of the American Revolution: How Common People Shaped the Fight for Independence* (New York: The New Press, 2001), p. 135.

4. Wayne Bodle, *The Valley Forge Winter: Civilians and Soldiers in War* (University Park: The Pennsylvania State University Press, 2002), p. 17.

5. Sally Smith Booth, *The Women of '76* (New York: Hastings House, 1973), p. 183.

6. Raphael, p. 124.

7. Berkin, p. 57.

8. Raphael, p. 120.

9. Thomas Fleming, *Washington's Secret War: The Hidden History of Valley Forge* (New York: HarperCollins, 2005), p. 185.

10. Cokie Roberts, *Founding Mothers: The Women Who Raised Our Nation* (New York: HarperCollins, 2004), p. 87.

11. Raphael, p. 124.

CHAPTER 4: AT THE BATTLEFRONT

1. Carol Berkin, *Revolutionary Mothers: Women in the Struggle for America's Independence* (New York: Knopf, 2005), p. xi.

2. Ibid., pp. 138–139.

3. Cokie Roberts, *Founding Mothers: The Women Who Raised Our Nation* (New York: HarperCollins, 2004), p. 82.

4. Sally Smith Booth, *The Women of '76* (New York: Hastings House, 1973), p. 268.

5. Ray Raphael, *A People's History of the American Revolution: How Common People Shaped the Fight for Independence* (New York: The New Press, 2001), p. 63.

6. John Greenwood, *A Young Patriot in the American Revolution* (n.p.: Westvaco, 1981), various pages.

7. Jim Murphy, *A Young Patriot: The American Revolution as Experienced by One Boy* (New York: Clarion, 1996), pp. 14–15.

8. Raphael, p. 62.

CHAPTER 5: SPIES AND MESSENGERS

1. Carol Berkin, *Revolutionary Mothers: Women in the Struggle for America's Independence* (New York: Knopf, 2005), p. 139.

2. Ibid., p. 142.

3. Ibid., pp. 143–144.

4. Ibid., p. 145.

5. Thomas Fleming, *Liberty! The American Revolution* (New York: Viking, 1997), p. 206.

6. Cokie Roberts, *Founding Mothers: The Women Who Raised Our Nation* (New York: HarperCollins, 2004), p. 80.

7. Sally Smith Booth, *The Women of '76* (New York: Hastings House, 1973), pp. 154–155.

8. Berkin, p. 141.

apprentice—A person who works for another to learn a trade.

boycott—To refuse to use certain goods or services, often as a form of protest.

camp follower—A woman or child who traveled with the army, often providing valuable services such as cooking and washing clothes.

cartridge—A paper tube containing a measured amount of gunpowder for use in firing a single round from a cannon or firearm.

cooper—A person who makes or repairs casks or barrels.

depot—A place where arms or supplies are stored.

discharge—To release a soldier from military service.

enlistment—The period of time a person is signed up for military service.

imported—Brought in from another source, usually another country.

livestock—Farm animals raised for food or other products, such as cattle, sheep, and pigs.

loyalist—An American who supported the British during the Revolutionary War.

militia—Citizens who enroll for military service. They drill from time to time but serve full time only in emergencies.

patriot—An American who was in favor of independence from Britain.

pension—A fixed amount paid at regular times for past service.

GLOSSARY

plantation—a large farm or estate on which crops such as cotton or tobacco are grown.

quota—A goal or assignment of goods to be produced.

rations—An allowance of food for civilians or soldiers during time of war.

saber—A heavy, one-edged sword.

sanitation—A system set up to ensure cleanliness and the disposal of waste.

skirmish—A fight between small units of armies, as opposed to a full battle.

spinster—An unmarried woman, usually beyond the age when most women are married.

spouse—A husband or wife.

BOOKS

Allen, Thomas B. *George Washington, Spymaster: How the Americans Outspied the British and Won the Revolutionary War.* Washington, D.C.: National Geographic Children's Books, 2007.

Beller, Susan Provost. *Yankee Doodle and the Redcoats: Soldiering in the Revolutionary War.* Minneapolis: Lerner, 2007.

St. George, Judith. *Betsy Ross: Patriot of Philadelphia.* New York: Henry Holt, 2007.

INTERNET ADDRESSES

The Betsy Ross Homepage

http://www.ushistory.org/betsy/

Kid Info: American Revolution

http://www.kidinfo.com/American_History/American_Revolution.html

Kids Konnect: American Revolution

http://www.kidskonnect.com/content/view/251/27/

Women and the American Revolution

http://womenshistory.about.com/od/waramrevolution/Women_and_the_American_Revolution.htm

FURTHER READING

Numbers in **bold italics** refer to captions.